STARBUCKS COFFEE ®

STARBUCKS *Passion* FOR COFFEE

A Starbucks Coffee Cookbook

Text by
DAVE OLSEN

Original Recipes by
JOHN PHILLIP CARROLL AND LORA BRODY

Sunset Books

President and Publisher: Susan J. Maruyama
Director, Finance & Business Affairs:
  Gary Loebner
Director, Manufacturing & Sales Service:
  Lorinda Reichert
Western Regional Sales Director:
  Richard A. Smeby
Eastern Regional Sales Director:
  Richard M. Miller
Editorial Director: Kenneth Winchester

Sunset Publishing Corporation

Chairman: Robert L. Miller
President/CEO: Robin Wolaner
Chief Financial Officer: James E. Mitchell
Publisher, Sunset Magazine: Stephen J. Seabolt
Circulation Director: Robert L. Gursha
Editor, Sunset Magazine: William R. Marken

Starbucks Passion for Coffee
was produced by
Weldon Owen, Inc.

President: John Owen
Publisher: Jane Fraser
Managing Editor: Anne Dickerson
Editorial Assistant: Jan Hughes
Art Direction and Design: John Bull
Design and Layout: Nancy Campana
Layout: Ruth Jacobson
Production: Stephanie Sherman
Map: Kenn Backhaus
Illustrators: Tracey Hughes,
  Todd Connor, Julia LaPine
Copy Editor: Judith Dunham
Proofreader: Sharilyn Hovind
Index: Ken Dellapenta
Writer: Norman Kolpas
Food Photography: Philip Salaverry
Food Stylist: Sue White
Assistant Food Stylists: Jennifer Spiegel,
  Bruce Yim
Prop Stylist: Amy Glenn
Assistant to Photographer: David Williams

First printing August 1994
Copyright © 1994 Starbucks Corporation
Published by Sunset Publishing
Corporation, Menlo Park, CA 94025.
First edition. All rights reserved, including
the right of reproduction in whole or
in part in any form.

ISBN 0-376-02613-8
Library of Congress Catalog Card
Number: 94-67315
Printed in the United States

For more information on *Starbucks
Passion for Coffee* or any other Sunset
Book, call 1-800-634-3095. For special
sales, bulk orders, and premium sales
information, call Sunset Custom Publishing
Services at (415) 324-5577.

Starbucks by mail. Call 1-800-782-7282 for
a free catalog subscription and information
on how to acquire Starbucks coffee.

 printed on recycled paper

Café de Flore, Paris

CONTENTS

Pursuing a Personal Passion

I had no idea what I was getting into. In the mid-1970s, life offered me a chance that I didn't fully understand until several years later. I had always been enticed by the aroma of coffee—intense, complex, like nothing else—and somehow found myself building an espresso coffee bar in the garage space of a former mortuary in Seattle, simply because I didn't know what to do instead.

Looking at Seattle now, it's hard to imagine a time when opening a coffee bar was a unique idea. I have since turned Cafe Allegro over to new and capable hands, but my early experiences there turned my life—personal as well as professional—in the direction of coffee, which I had until then taken for granted. With all of its apparent contradictions—mysterious yet comforting, dark yet enlightening, seductive and stimulating, wonderfully complex and an everyday pleasure—coffee became a passion for me.

Now I know that I had simply stepped into a stream of coffee history that had been flowing for centuries. The feeling of discovery and invention that I felt initially, as I explored espresso—the very soul of coffee—expanded to a deepening appreciation of coffee in all its aspects. Most recently, as Starbucks' green coffee buyer, I have had intimate exposure to everything that matters in the world of coffee, from the handsome evergreen coffee trees and the farmers who tend them to the many ways to prepare coffee and the people who love to drink it. I am thankful that I have the opportunity to spend my life in such a business and I expect that there will be such opportunities for many years to come, both for me and for others whom coffee chooses to entice.

When he learned what business I was in, a soft-spoken Italian man now living in the U.S. told me, very seriously, that he hoped I understood the responsibility that came with coffee: "Coffee is what makes civilized life possible in these demanding times." A "coffee break" is a welcome and clearly understood time-out from a tedious task. Making a "coffee date" stands safely in the middle between a wish and the real thing. Coffee at breakfast, coffee with chocolate, coffee shops, coffee klatches all speak to the many conventions that surround coffee drinking.

So here is a coffee *book,* which I hope you find enjoyable and informative. Mainly, I hope it helps you to appreciate a little more the coffee you already enjoy, and to find *new* ways to enjoy great coffee and the foods that go well with it.

DAVE OLSEN
senior vice president, coffee; Starbucks Coffee Company

A PASSION FOR COFFEE

I've always been intrigued by attempts to explain how our passion for coffee first ignited over 1,500 years ago. Legends abound, but I like to think of coffee's discovery on a much more personal level—a level you or I can immediately appreciate. Imagine yourself on the high Ethiopian plains where coffee first grew. Lightning strikes a tree filled with coffee cherries. A rich, smoky perfume rises from the burning shrub and grabs your attention. Or maybe you've plucked some of those ripe, red cherries to enjoy their tantalizing sweet pulp, then tossed the seeds into a campfire. You can't believe the aroma that bursts forth.

Undoubtedly the smell of freshly roasted beans beguiled the world's first coffee drink-ers. That won-drous aroma first excited my passion for coffee —and very likely yours, too.

View of Mt. Remuk, East Java   **7**

The Coffeehouse Experience

Savored as it is from first sip to last, and reviving as it is to the mind and senses, coffee is a wonderful source of both private pleasure and social stimulation. This explains why and how coffee drinking spread worldwide, its growing popularity forever linked to the coffeehouse.

Well before the 13th century, coffeehouses were fixtures of Middle Eastern life. By the end of the 17th century, they also thrived in Italy, France, Austria, Germany, Holland, England and elsewhere. From time to time, rulers, politicians and religious leaders—from Prussia's Frederick the Great to England's King Charles II to Pope Clement VIII—tried to close coffeehouses, wanting to put an end to the free-spirited discussions they encouraged. But the coffeehouse always prevailed. Explorers and traders went on to spread coffee cultivation eastward to Indonesia and westward to the Caribbean and Latin America. And European settlers carried coffee drinking with them to the New World.

Today, as they first did more than 700 years ago, coffeehouses offer a delightful diversity of experiences. You can chat with friends, join in heated discussions or read in solitude. You can study, sketch or write. You can listen to music or hear poetry recited. You can play cards, checkers, backgammon, chess. As an unsung Viennese wit once put it, a coffeehouse is "the ideal place for people who want to be alone but need company for it."

All the while, whatever you choose to do, you can sip and enjoy one of the world's great pleasures.

Parisians enjoying the café life

Turkish coffee kiosk in Constantinople (now Istanbul), overlooking the Bosporus

A Sip of History

In the eastern Mediterranean and Middle East, coffee is prepared and enjoyed much as it probably was in coffee-houses almost 1,000 years ago.

Referred to generally as Turkish coffee, such a cup may be brewed easily at home in any small saucepan—and all the more easily if you have an *ibrik,* the traditional long-handled, tapered brass or copper Turkish coffeepot.

For each demitasse-sized cup, put 3 ounces of cold water in a saucepan or *ibrik* and bring to a boil over low heat.

For each serving, stir in 1 heaping teaspoon of espresso-grind Arabian Mocha Sanani or other Arabian beans and about 1 teaspoon of sugar or an amount that suits your taste.

When the coffee boils up to a thick, high froth, remove the pot from the heat and stir. Repeat the boiling, frothing and stirring once more.

Boil the coffee a third time and, when the froth builds, spoon a small amount of coffee into each preheated cup for good luck. Then fill the cups and serve immediately.

Coffee is the common man's gold, and like gold, it brings to every man the feeling of luxury and nobility.

Abd-al-Kadir, *In Praise of Coffee,* 1587

To the Coffee House!

When you are worried, have trouble of one sort or
 another—to the coffee house!
When she did not keep her appointment, for one reason
 or other—to the coffee house!
When your shoes are torn and dilapidated—coffee house!
When your income is four hundred crowns and you spend
 five hundred—coffee house!
You are a chair warmer in some office, while your ambition
 led you to seek professional honors—coffee house!
You could not find a mate to suit you—coffee house!
You feel like committing suicide—coffee house!
You hate and despise human beings, and at the same time
 you can not be happy without them—coffee house!
You compose a poem which you can not inflict upon friends
 you meet in the street—coffee house!
When your coal scuttle is empty, and your gas ration
 exhausted—coffee house!
When you are locked out and haven't the money to pay for
 unlocking the house door—coffee house!
When you acquire a new flame, and intend provoking the
 old one, you take the new one to the old one's—
 coffee house!
When you feel like hiding, you dive into a—coffee house!
When you want to be seen in a new suit—coffee house!
When you can not get anything on trust anywhere else—
 coffee house!

Viennese poet Peter Altenberg, quoted in
All About Coffee, *1922, by William H. Ukers*

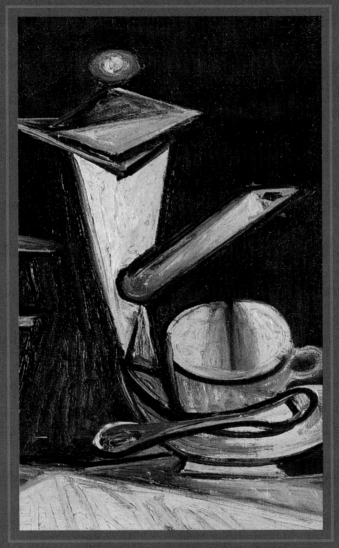

Pablo Picasso, The Coffee Pot, *1945–46, oil on canvas*

Coffee and Culture

Throughout the history of coffee, great artists, writers, musicians and thinkers have gravitated to the coffeehouse. Their creative expression, briefly sampled here, reflects coffee's gift of inspiration.

Literature

Poets from John Milton (1608–1674) to Alexander Pope (1688–1744) to John Keats (1795–1821), dramatists from Voltaire (1694–1778) to Carlo Goldoni (1707–1793) and novelists from Honoré de Balzac (1799–1850) to Mark Twain (1835–1910) to D. H. Lawrence (1885–1930) have sustained their imaginations with cups of coffee and sung its praises in their works.

Balzac offered one of literature's most vivid descriptions of coffee's inspiring and rousing effect in his "Treatise on Modern Stimulants":

> *This coffee falls into your stomach, and straightway there is a general commotion. Ideas begin to move like the battalions of the Grand Army on the battlefield, and the battle takes place. Things remembered arrive at full gallop, ensign to the wind. The light cavalry of comparisons deliver a magnificent deploying charge, the artillery of logic hurry up with their train and ammunition, the shafts of wit start up like sharpshooters. Similes arise, the paper is covered with ink; for the struggle commences and is concluded with torrents of black water, just as a battle with powder.*

Music

From "Let's Have Another Cup of Coffee" by Irving Berlin (1888–1989) to other standards like "Coffee in the Morning and Kisses in the Night," "You're the Cream in My Coffee" and "The Java Jive," the popular brew has been celebrated repeatedly in the world of popular music.

None other than Ludwig van Beethoven (1770–1827), though he never paid musical tribute to coffee, was said to take special pains over the preparation of his daily brew—carefully counting out 60 roasted beans for every cup.

Philosophy

German metaphysical philosopher Immanuel Kant (1724–1804) was so devoted to his after-dinner cup that, in the final year of his life, he was heard to mutter the following complaint when his coffee was late in arriving: "Well, one can die after all; it is but dying; and in the next world, thank God, there is no drinking of coffee and consequently no waiting for it."

PLANTATION TO CUP

Exploring the World of Coffee

One of the greatest pleasures of my own work comes in visiting the many countries where coffee is grown, in search of the world's best. You can join me without ever leaving home, simply by sampling the beans I bring back.

I'll introduce you to varietal coffees from the many origin countries of East Africa and Arabia, Indonesia and the Americas. Our explorations of what happens when you blend two or more coffees together will enhance your pleasure even more. Along the way, you'll also learn an important yet profoundly simple lesson of the coffee world, one that I hope will come to guide you in your choice of the coffee you buy and the way you brew it: *Everything matters.*

The journey doesn't cost much, but the rewards are priceless. So pack your cup and come along!

Harvesting coffee, Colombia

The Coffee Belt

Encircling the world, within the tropical latitudes, is a narrow belt—the coffee belt. This tropical region supports the coffee tree, which requires abundant sunshine, moderate rainfall, year-round warm temperatures averaging 70°F and no frost.

Two species of coffee tree produce coffees of commercial importance. The robusta is, as the name implies, a robust species, resistant to disease, with a high yield per plant. Flourishing at low elevations, it produces harsh coffees that are also high in caffeine. The arabica, which accounts for about 75 percent of world production, thrives in volcanic soil at high altitudes of 3,000 to 6,500 feet. Arabica yields the world's best coffees, more refined than robusta coffees, with a caffeine level less than half that of robusta beans. The slower growing cycle of arabica coffee trees at higher elevations concentrates still more flavor in the beans, producing some of the finest of all coffees—so-called high-grown beans.

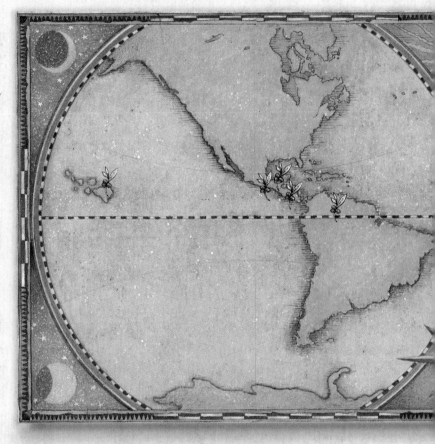

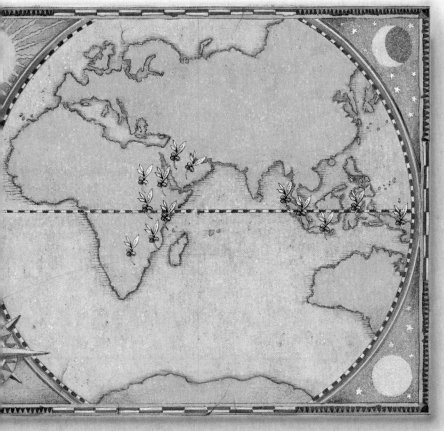

The World's Coffee Families

Many nations within the coffee belt produce fine arabica coffees. While coffees will differ from one country or area to the next, depending on growing conditions and preparation methods, those in each general coffee-growing region in the world exhibit common characteristics that you can learn to recognize, linking them in a geographic coffee "family."

East Africa and Arabia —

Denotes major coffee growing areas.

Beans from the region that gave birth to coffee generally have rich flavor, sparkling acidity, unique floral or winy qualities, and medium to full body. Included in this family are coffees from Burundi, Ethiopia, Kenya, Malawi, Tanzania, Uganda, Yemen, Zambia and Zimbabwe.

Indonesia and the Pacific — Dutch traders spread coffee cultivation to Indonesia by the late 17th century. These coffees are usually smooth, earthy and exotic-tasting, with low acidity and full body. The family includes coffees from Java, Sulawesi (Celebes) and Sumatra. Coffee from Papua New Guinea, while geographically related, has a spicier, more pointed flavor with brighter acidity—an exception to the family rule.

Americas — The French, Dutch and Portuguese began cultivating coffee here in the 1720s. Today's best coffees from this family are clean-tasting and lively, with light to medium body. Included in this group are Colombia, Costa Rica, Guatemala, Honduras, Jamaica, Mexico, Nicaragua and Panama as well as coffee from Kona, the southwestern coast of the island of Hawaii.

Coffee Beans: From Tree to Roaster

Wherever in the world high-quality coffee is grown, it follows
a similar journey to reach a coffee roaster's warehouse. Yet,
every step of the way, subtle variations in that journey will
affect the inherent characteristics and
quality of the coffee that you
finally drink. In short,
everything matters.

*Botanical rendering of a
branch from an Arabian coffee tree
and detailed illustrations of the
flower, cherries and beans, 1801*

The Coffee Tree

Most often called a tree, the plant that gives us coffee is actually a tropical evergreen shrub with delicate white blossoms whose intense fragrance resembles that of jasmine. The "beans" are, in fact, the seeds or pits of the fruit—known as coffee cherries for their plumpness and ripe red color. Each cherry normally contains two beans, which grow with their flat sides facing each other. An exception is the so-called peaberry, a rounded bean that grows one to a cherry.

It usually takes about five years for a coffee tree to bear its first full crop, at which stage it will have grown and been pruned to maintain a height of about 6 feet. The tree can continue to be productive for 15 years or more, annually producing enough cherries to yield about one pound of roasted coffee.

Not all coffee cherries ripen at the same time, and any branch of a tree might simultaneously bear blossoms, green fruit and ripe cherries. So quality coffees must be picked entirely by hand, a process that requires three or four visits per tree each year. In one day, an experienced coffee plantation worker can pick up to 200 pounds of ripe cherries, equivalent to about 50 pounds of green coffee beans.

Small starburst-shaped coffee flowers eventually give way to cherries.

Wet and Dry Processing

Once the cherries have been picked, the beans must be extracted from them. The task may be accomplished by one of two different methods, determined by the availability of water in the region where the coffee is grown. The wet method, used in major Latin American coffee countries (except Brazil) and in other regions, requires abundant fresh water. A machine first strips away the outer layers of skin and fruity pulp. The beans, still tightly enclosed in a sticky inner pulp and a tight parchment wrapper, are soaked for 24 to 72 hours in large fermentation tanks. This process loosens the fruity pulp, which is washed away. The beans are then dried in the sun or in mechanical driers. The resulting beans, sometimes known as "washed" coffees, generally will have higher acidity and cleaner, more consistent flavors than beans processed by the dry method.

In the dry, or "natural," method, coffee cherries are spread out to dry in the sun for two to three weeks. When the fruit has dried, a hulling machine strips away the outer skin and pulp. Though the results are not always consistent in quality, the acidity of the beans is reduced and the body increased. Many of the world's greatest

Careful hand-picking yields uniformly ripe coffee cherries.

coffees—including Arabian Mocha and many Indonesian varietals—are processed by this method.

After wet or dry processing, a mill removes any remnants of the parchment along with the silverskin, a tissue-thin covering that clings to the beans. The beans are then carefully sorted by hand and machine to remove defects and to separate them by size before they are bagged, graded for quality and readied for sale.

Beans drying in the sun, Guatemala

Cuptesting

The quality and consistency of a sample of coffee beans is ultimately judged through "cuptesting" or "cupping," a ritualized and scientific process as simple but as exacting as wine tasting.

Coffee specialists take a small sample from each lot of beans they consider for purchase. In a small countertop roasting machine, the sample is first roasted. Two tablespoons of coarsely ground beans from the sample are then placed in each of several glass or porcelain cups, which are then filled with 6 ounces of water just off the boil.

The coffee taster then moves his or her nose close to the cup and uses

In the tasting room at Starbucks' Seattle headquarters, Dave Olsen utilizes all of his five senses when sampling coffee.

the back of a silver or stainless-steel spoon to break the crust of grounds on the surface. The resulting burst of aroma is noted. After the grounds steep and settle, the cups are skimmed and allowed to cool slightly. Then the coffee taster noisily sips a spoonful of coffee, at the same time sucking in air through pursed lips to aerate the coffee, thus engaging the senses of both taste and smell. The spoonful is spat out before the next sample is tasted.

Tasters keep notes on general and specific impressions of each coffee's flavor, acidity and body, and of the consistency of these characteristics from one cup to the next. Few samples meet the standards of a high-quality roaster like Starbucks, where very few of several hundred samples tasted each year are judged good enough to be considered for purchase.

The Art of Roasting

The world's best coffee beans realize their full potential only through careful batch roasting—a process monitored and adjusted constantly by a skilled roasting expert. Over the course of 11 to 15 minutes, depending on the individual batch, the temperature of the beans rises to as high as 450°F. Their color progresses from straw-green, to yellow-orange, to light cinnamon (the maximum degree of roasting that can be withstood by beans destined for lesser-quality commercial coffees), to an optimal rich chestnut brown. The color is allowed to turn darker still for espresso and Italian and French roasts. Along the way, the beans pop open, doubling in size while losing about 18 percent of their weight in a Starbucks Roast™ and up to 25 percent of their weight in a French roast.

The most important transformation occurs in the volatile flavor oils of the coffee beans. The oils gradually develop to the critical point in a Starbucks Roast™ at which their varietal character is fully realized, with every flavor element in perfect balance. At that precise moment—ultimately judged through the roasting expert's eyes, ears and nose—the beans are released into a rotating cooling tray. In just 4 minutes, powerful fans draw off their heat, and the beans darken one final shade as they swirl around hypnotically, crackling with heavenly aroma.

A rich-smelling haze of smoke rises from coffee beans as they are released from a batch roaster into a cooling tray at the Starbucks roasting plant.

Flavor Development During Roasting

GREEN
Raw Beans

In their raw state, coffee beans look like inert green pebbles, their flavor potential locked deep within.

CITY ROAST
Acidity dominates body

At 10 to 11 minutes, the beans reach an even, light brown, developing a full flavor dominated by markedly high acidity. Many specialty coffee companies use this roast—some well, some poorly.

YELLOW
Moisture Loss

After 5 to 7 minutes, the beans begin to lose moisture and turn yellow-orange. Yellow beans exude a distinctive aroma, often compared to buttery vegetables.

STARBUCKS ROAST™
Fully Ripe

After 11 to 15 minutes, the beans turn a rich chestnut brown. At this stage, their acids and sugars are uniquely balanced, and their full varietal character has been realized.

CINNAMON ROAST
Beans pop open

The beans increase in size and turn a light tan. Sour "green" flavors predominate, and body and complexity remain undeveloped. This stage is sometimes called an "institutional roast."

DARK ROASTS
Caramelly and Spicy to Pungent and Smoky

Dark…Darker…Darkest. Dark roast: the flavor becomes focused, rich and sweet; natural sugars caramelize, making this roast ideal for espresso. A bit darker, and oils come to the surface, producing a sweet but lighter bodied cup. Finally, pushed to the limit, beans turn dark and shiny, taking on an intense, smoky flavor.

Tasting Terminology

So many adjectives apply to the taste of coffee that descriptions of specific varietals and blends can begin to resemble poetry. Such words are subjective, and whatever descriptions work best for you are fine.

The Basics

In describing your own response to coffee-tasting experiences, it might help to bear in mind the three fundamental aspects of any coffee's taste.

Flavor

The most important tasting term describes the total impression of aroma, acidity and body. It can be used generally ("this coffee is flavorful") or with specific attributes in mind ("this coffee has a flavor reminiscent of chocolate").

Acidity

This easily misunderstood term refers to the lively, palate-cleansing property characteristic of all high-grown coffees, which is experienced primarily on the sides of the tongue. Acidity is not the same as bitterness.

Body

The tactile impression of brewed coffee in your mouth can be described as light, medium or full. Some coffees naturally have more body than others. The brewing method also affects the perception of body. Coffees made in a French press (page 36) or an espresso machine (page 42) seem fuller in body than those brewed by other methods.

(page 36); (page 42)

Aroma Fragrance of brewed coffee. **Earthy** Spicy taste "of the earth," often used to describe Indonesian coffees. **Exotic** Applied to coffees with an unusual aroma or flavor suggestive of flowers, berries or sweet spices, for example. **Mellow** Well-balanced coffee of low to medium acidity. **Mild** Denotes coffee with harmonious flavor, such as high-grown Latin American coffees. **Soft** Low-acid coffees such as Indonesians, which may also be called mellow or sweet. **Spicy** Describes an aroma or flavor reminiscent of a particular spice. **Sweet** Smooth and palatable. **Tangy** Denotes a darting, pleasing brightness. **Wild** Racy nuances of flavor, as found in Ethiopia Harrar. **Winy** Fruitlike acidity and smooth body reminiscent of fine red wine.

A Chart to Guide You on Your Coffee Journey

The freshly roasted beans you buy from a coffee roaster dedicated to quality will reflect all the care that went into their growing, processing, selection and roasting. The coffee you brew from them, following a few simple principles (pages 32–33), will bring you great pleasure.

One of the greatest pleasures to be had from drinking quality coffee, perfectly brewed, is that of discovery: exploring the diversity of tastes that exist in varietal coffees—those from specific growers, areas or countries—and in blends of two or more different kinds of varietal beans. You can chart your journey through the coffees of the world in any way you desire—by delving into one region in depth, methodically circumnavigating the globe or even wandering from country to country with no set plan.

But to build your understanding more systematically, you might consider gradually progressing from the straightforward coffee experiences to those that are more complex and intriguing—wherever they might be found. Let the following chart be your guide. Its brief descriptions of select high-quality coffee varietals—as sold by a quality roaster—can serve as starting points for making your own discoveries and developing your personal impressions of the coffee you drink.

Lively Experiences
Bright, Mild and Welcoming

Kona
Smooth, gentle and mild.

Mexico Altura
Light and lively, with a delicate nutty flavor.

Costa Rica Tres Rios
Lively, fragrant and tangy, with a morning brightness.

Ethiopia Sidamo
Sweet flavor and floral aroma.

Ethiopia Yergacheffe
Medium-bodied, with sweet flavor and aroma.

Tanzania
Clean and direct flavor, with a brisk liveliness.

Rich Traditions
Deep, Complex and Satisfying

Guatemala Antigua
Complex and refined, with hints of cocoa and spice.

Colombia Nariño Supremo
Unusually full-bodied, with a walnut flavor.

Papua New Guinea
Rich, harmoniously pungent and tangy, with medium body.

Kenya
Bright, rich and sweet, with a hint of black currant.

Zimbabwe
Sparkling, piquant and well-balanced, with a spicy aftertaste.

Bold Expressions
Diverse, Distinctive and Intriguing

Ethiopia Harrar
Earthy and exotic, with an intense berrylike flavor.

Arabian Mocha Sanani
Wild, pungent and winy, exotically spicy and sweet.

Estate Java
Full-bodied, syrupy, powerful and peppery.

Sumatra
Full-bodied, syrupy, deep and earthy.

Sulawesi
Smooth and buttery, with well-rounded flavor and rich aroma.

Coffee Blends

Just as an artist can combine two or more colors on a palette to produce a vibrant, distinctive hue, so high-quality coffee roasters can combine different varietal beans in varying proportions to make blends that offer a more complex, complete coffee-drinking experience than the mere sums of their parts.

A successful blend might contrast the acidity of a Central American coffee with the smoothness of Indonesian beans, for example, or might include dark Italian-roasted beans for extra depth and sweetness. Or coffees from several different countries might be carefully blended for the definitive experience of a particular region. The Starbucks Gazebo Blend®, for example, might combine beans from Kenya, Ethiopia, Malawi, Burundi, Tanzania, Zambia, Zimbabwe or Yemen, yielding a blend whose clean, crisp taste is ideal, hot or cold, for summertime sipping. The Starbucks Christmas Blend® marries Central American and rare Indonesian varietals, including aged Indonesians, for a subtle, spicy, mellow flavor and robust body perfectly suited to the holiday season.

The world's best-known blend is undoubtedly Arabian Mocha Java. Full-bodied, spicy Estate Java beans combine perfectly with pungent, aromatic Arabian Mocha beans to produce a powerful, yet well-balanced brew that stands as an archetypal coffee-drinking experience, honoring the tradition of the first-ever coffee blend.

You might wish to experiment with your own blends, combining different favorite varietals in just the right proportions to give you a cup that precisely suits your personal taste. Start with a base of one coffee that you know well and enjoy. Then add one or more other coffees for more depth, richness, body or complexity. Bear in mind that blending is both art and science, and some of your experiments might not yield the results you hope for.

Here are some blend recommendations to get you started:

50 percent Sumatra, 50 percent Sulawesi: earthy and refined
50 percent Java, 50 percent Guatemala: full-bodied and complex
75 percent Sulawesi, 25 percent Italian roast: elegant and sweet

Literally months of trial and error in roasting, tasting and combining different varietal coffees are required to create a truly special coffee blend.

COFFEE BREWING

Brewing Perfect Coffee at Home

With just 50 to 75 individual beans of your favorite coffee variety or blend, expertly roasted to develop their full character, very little stands in the way of your enjoying a great cup of coffee. I think I've tried all the brewing methods, and most are described in the pages that follow. My personal favorites are press pots and all kinds of espresso machines; other methods have their benefits, too.

Fortunately, in each case, great coffee is easier to make than a great omelette, or even than great scrambled eggs. Brewing perfect coffee is perfectly simple. Here at Starbucks, we sum up the secret of success with Four Fundamentals: proportion, grind, water and freshness. Here's a phrase to make them easier to remember: *Please Go With Fundamentals!*

The Four Fundamentals

Think of coffee making as a form of cooking.
Naturally you want to start with the best ingredients: the better the beans,
the better the cup. Following a tested, proven recipe, you then need to
prepare them in the right way and in the correct proportions. Once the
recipe is completed, you want to enjoy the coffee at its peak of perfection.
Such is the simple logic that supports the Four Fundamentals.
Understand and follow each of them, and brew perfect coffee every time.

Proportion – Use the right proportion of coffee to water.

This is the most important step in making perfect coffee. You need 2 tablespoons of ground coffee for every 6 ounces of water.

Time and experience have borne out these proportions as ideal for a full-flavored cup of coffee (though you can feel free, after using them for about a week, to adjust the proportions to your own taste). An approved coffee measure, a plastic scoop (sold in Starbucks stores) that measures precisely 2 tablespoons of ground coffee, delivers the perfect proportions. Bear in mind that many home coffeemakers come with scoops that hold only 1 tablespoon, half the required measure for 6 ounces of water—a surefire recipe for weak coffee.

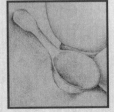

Grind – Use the right grind of coffee for your coffeemaker.

How finely or coarsely your coffee is ground determines how quickly water will pass through it. Different brewing methods, as shown on pages 36–39, require different grinds, depending on how long they allow the water to remain in contact with the ground coffee. A grind that is too coarse for the method you use lets the water pass through too quickly, yielding under-extracted, watery coffee. A grind that is too fine for your method allows the water too much contact with the ground beans, extracting flavor compounds that produce a bitter cup of coffee.

A blade grinder, whose twin stainless-steel cutting surfaces whirl and chop coffee beans ever finer the longer you process them, does a good job—though you have to pay careful attention to get the right grind. Even better is a burr-type grinder, which uniformly grinds coffee beans to whatever degree you set.

Water – Use fresh, cold water, just off a boil.

The water you use will affect the flavor of the coffee you make with it. After all, coffee is 98 percent water. Avoid water from a water softener, city water that tastes like chlorine, well water that tastes like iron or sulfur—or any water with a strong flavor. If your local tap water has no unpleasant flavors, feel free to use it. Otherwise, make your coffee with filtered or bottled water.

Water just off the boil—195°–205°F—extracts just the right amount of flavor from ground coffee. Any cooler and it can't adequately extract the coffee's complete range of flavors.

An automatic coffeemaker heats the water for you; make sure that the one you buy gets the water hot enough. When using a pot or kettle to heat water, bring the water to a boil. Then remove it from the heat and wait a few seconds before you pour it over the ground coffee.

Freshness – Start with freshly roasted coffee beans, freshly ground, then drink the coffee freshly brewed.

Fresh coffee beans should be used within two weeks of purchase from a reputable roaster or retailer. If you can, buy your coffee weekly. If you must store it for more than two weeks, keep the beans in the freezer in the smallest practical airtight container.

Coffee's main enemies are oxygen and moisture. To maintain freshness, store it in an airtight container at cool room temperature, away from light. Make the small investment in a grinder so you can grind the beans every time you make coffee. Ground coffee will stay fresh only for a few days.

For the best coffee, brew it fresh every time you serve it. Keep it on a warmer or, better yet, put it in a thermos. Never reheat coffee or let it sit on a warmer for more than 20 minutes. At best, it will taste dull and stale; at worst, it will develop a bitter, acrid flavor.

Basic Brewing Methods

Following the Four Fundamentals explained on the previous pages, you can brew excellent coffee by any of several methods. Each, in its way, will produce slightly different results. Select a method that will give you the kind of coffee you most enjoy drinking. Then, for that particular method, buy brewing equipment that best meets the Four Fundamentals.

An Iced Coffee Tip

In hot weather, a glass of iced coffee can be especially refreshing. But ice cubes dilute the full flavor of coffee brewed in the usual way.

One way to make good iced coffee is to brew it double-strength in a press (page 36), using twice the usual proportion of coffee to water. As soon as it is ready, pour the coffee into a pitcher completely filled with ice cubes, which will partially melt as they chill the coffee, giving the proper dilution.

Or, you might like to keep in your freezer a stock of ice cubes made from coffee, ready to chill regular-strength coffee.

The Press

This traditional French-style coffeemaker lets coarsely ground coffee steep in boiled water for 4 minutes. Its plunger-style metal rod then pushes a fine-meshed stainless-steel screen—tightly held against the edge of the cylindrical pot by a spring—down through the liquid, forcing the grounds to the bottom of the pot.

The resulting coffee is rich and flavorful, with a fine sediment that makes it feel thick and full-bodied in the mouth.

Press pots, whether made of tempered glass or pottery, look elegant on the dining table, but they cannot be placed on a warmer to reheat the coffee.

Follow this procedure for making coffee in a press:

- Clean the pot and plunger assembly thoroughly with hot, soapy water.
- Rinse the plunger assembly and pot with hot water to preheat them.
- Measure into the pot the right amount of coarsely ground coffee: 2 tablespoons for each 6 ounces of water.
- Add water just off the boil and stir to mix. Place the plunger assembly loosely on top to hold in the heat. Steep 4 minutes.
- Pointing the pouring spout away from you and holding the pot by the handle, slowly press the plunger down with your other hand to force the grounds to the bottom of the pot. Serve immediately.

In eras past, coffee was ground in a hand-cranked mill—a task, along with brewing, reserved for servants. In his book *Mr. Sammler's Planet* (1970), Saul Bellow poignantly captures a moment of historical transition, when household staff was a thing of the past and convenient electric grinders awaited in the future.

> *Mr. Sammler ground his coffee in a square box, cranking counterclockwise between long knees. To commonplace actions he brought a special pedantic awkwardness. In Poland, France, England, students, young gentlemen of his time, had been unacquainted with kitchens. Now he did things that cooks and maids had once done. He did them with a certain priestly stiffness. Acknowledgment of social descent. Historical ruin. Transformation of society. It was beyond personal humbling.*

But Mr. Sammler's coffee was still all the better for the grinding!

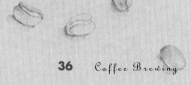

The Drip Filter

In this popular brewing method, a cone-shaped or flat-bottomed filter holds ground coffee in a plastic or pottery basket set on top of a serving pot or an individual cup or mug. Water, heated automatically or by a hand-held kettle, drips through the ground coffee into the pot below.

The result is a clean-tasting, full-flavored cup of coffee. When made with a disposable paper filter, the coffee is free of sediment and therefore seems lighter in body than coffee made in a press. A gold-plated permanent filter (see sidebar) allows more flavor and a bit of sediment to pass through, without passing along any taste, unlike a paper filter.

The tempered glass carafes of most drip coffeemakers allow the coffee to be kept warm. If you are considering an electric drip coffeemaker, seek out a model that heats the water to the proper brewing temperature. It should also have a warming burner that shuts off after 20 minutes, ensuring freshness.

Follow this procedure for making coffee using the drip method:

◉ Automatic Drip: Fill the reservoir with cold, fresh water. Manual Drip: Fill a kettle and bring the water to a boil.

◉ Automatic or Manual: Place a filter paper or a gold-plated permanent filter in the filter basket. Measure the right amount of coffee—fine grind for cone-shaped filters, medium grind for most flat-bottomed filters—into the filter: 2 tablespoons for each 6 ounces of water.

◉ Automatic: Turn on the coffeemaker. Manual: Slowly pour the right amount of water, just off the boil, over the coffee.

◉ Automatic or Manual: When all the water has dripped through, briefly stir the pot because the coffee at the bottom will be slightly stronger than the last coffee to have dripped through the filter. Serve immediately.

THE GOLD STANDARD

Lovers of drip coffee who wish to avoid the inconvenience and expense of filter papers, or who desire a somewhat richer flavor, should seek out a gold filter.

Made of high-density plastic coated with 23-karat gold, the filter is sold in both conical and flat-bottomed shapes. Unlike paper, it does not soak up some of coffee's essential oils and therefore allows more flavor to pass into the pot. The fine mesh also permits a slight bit of pleasurable sediment to pass through.

To clean the filter, simply discard the wet grounds and rinse the filter by hand with mild soap and water. To avoid wearing away the gold plating, do not scrub it or put it in the dishwasher.

The Cold-Water Brewer

Coffee lovers, because of personal taste or sensitive stomachs, may wish to eliminate much of the natural acidity from their coffee. They might therefore want to try a cold-water coffeemaker. The method, popular among Dutch settlers in Java in the 19th century, steeps coarsely ground coffee in cold, fresh water for up to 24 hours.

When filtered, the liquid concentrate may be stored in the refrigerator for up to one week or may be frozen for longer periods. When reconstituted, it results in a smooth-tasting, low-acid cup of coffee.

Follow this procedure for making coffee by the cold-water method:

❧ Soak the filter in a solution of baking soda and water, then rinse thoroughly with fresh water before use.

❧ Fit the filter in the cold-water brewing container, and place the stopper outside. Fill the container with 1 pound of coarsely ground coffee and 1 quart of cold, fresh water.

❧ Leave at room temperature to steep for 18 to 24 hours.

❧ Remove the stopper and place the container over its carafe, letting the concentrate slowly filter into the container.

❧ Store in the refrigerator up to one week, or transfer to a freezer-proof container and freeze.

❧ To reconstitute, for each serving add 2 ounces of concentrate for every 6 ounces of water just off the boil. Serve immediately.

The Vacuum Pot

Invented in 1840 by Scottish marine engineer Robert Napier, the vacuum method brews coffee that some people judge the best of all—a brew as full-flavored as that made in a French press, yet hotter and almost as clear and sediment-free as drip coffee. In fact, some fans of the vacuum pot say that it yields coffee that tastes just like it smells.

But a vacuum coffeemaker, which resembles laboratory glassware, is cumbersome and fragile, and requires painstaking attention and careful storage. That didn't hinder the pot's popularity during its heyday in the 1920s, '30s and '40s. Detective novelist Raymond Chandler made it the brewing method of choice for his private eye Philip Marlowe (see sidebar). Katharine Hepburn struggled with the vacuum pot to hilarious effect in the movie *Woman of the Year* (1942).

However, you don't have to struggle. Just follow this procedure for making coffee in a vacuum pot:

@ Fit the permanent filter above the central spout inside the upper bowl. Add the correct amount of finely ground coffee: 2 tablespoons for every 6 ounces of water.
@ Fill the lower bowl with fresh water. Bring the water to a boil and remove from the heat.
@ Secure the upper bowl onto the lower bowl, and return the pot to low heat. The water will rise from the lower bowl into the upper. Stir briefly and leave on the heat for 1 minute.
@ Remove the pot from the heat. As the pot cools, the vacuum formed in the lower bowl will slowly pull the brewed coffee down through the filter from the upper bowl—in 3 to 4 minutes. Remove the upper bowl and serve.

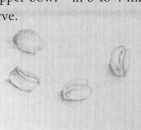

Espresso: The Soul of Coffee

A cup of well-made espresso offers a haunting glimpse into the very soul
of coffee. The experience is fragile and fleeting, yet intense and memorable:
a flow of *crema,* the soft, golden froth; an aroma that fills the room; a few sips
of hot, nectarlike liquid. Then it's gone, leaving only an exquisite aftertaste
and an indelible memory. The word *espresso* has a double meaning.
The first—"rapid"—comes from the Italians. In 1903 they invented the
method and machines for forcing hot water at high pressure through
very finely ground coffee, quickly yielding a cup of coffee. But the root
of the French word for espresso—*exprès*—highlights another
aspect of its charm: coffee made expressly for you.

Italy's Four M's of Perfect Espresso

Just as the Four Fundamentals (pages 32–33) guide you in
making the best coffee, so Italian tradition identifies four factors that
produce the perfect cup of espresso.

Miscela (mis-SHAY-la): Blend

Start with coffee beans selected and roasted to yield a thick, caramel-tasting,
aromatic cup. You can use a special blend of coffees—a mixture of Central
American and Indonesian beans, for example—or a varietal coffee such as
Guatemala Antigua, Ethiopia Yergacheffe, Arabian Mocha Sanani, Sumatra
or Sulawesi (pages 27–28).

Macinazione (MA-chee-na-tsee-onay): Grinding

A fine, powdery espresso grind allows water to flow through at a slow,
steady pace, for a cup of espresso with the best flavor and consistency.
Coffee should be freshly ground, since such a fine grind quickly loses its
flavor. It's a good idea to purchase a burr-type grinder, which allows you to
fine-tune your grind to your individual machine.

Macchina (MA-keen-a): Machine

Small countertop espresso machines make it possible to brew the authentic
drink at home. These, like their larger and far more expensive restaurant-
style cousins, force hot water through the coffee at high pressure using an
electric pump or a piston. Espresso makers designed for stovetop use yield
true espresso only with considerable difficulty; the more likely outcome is
double-strength coffee without the rich, creamy intensity.

Mano (MAH-no): Hand

The hand of a skilled operator ensures that each cup of espresso is brewed
to perfection. The right amount of ground coffee—known as the "dose"—
must be measured for the amount of espresso being brewed. For full extraction of flavor, the coffee must be tamped down just firmly enough to allow
water to flow slowly through it in a stream about as thin as the lead in a
pencil. The coffee should be carefully watched during extraction—with
the goal being 1 to 1½ ounces of liquid in about 20 seconds for a single
shot—and the pump should be turned off the instant this goal is achieved.

Home Espresso—Step by Step

Before using any manufacturer's home espresso machine, read the enclosed instructions carefully. You can also use the following basic steps to help you achieve success whatever method you use:

◉ Fill the machine's reservoir with cold, fresh water.

◉ Plug in the machine.

◉ Fill the filter basket with espresso-grind coffee, allowing a dose of approximately 1½ tablespoons for a single-shot, full-sized filter insert. Tamp the coffee down lightly but firmly. Clamp the filter securely into the machine and place a cup underneath.

◉ When the water is ready, flip the switch or push the button that starts the machine, forcing the hot water through the coffee.

◉ Turn off the machine when you have 1 to 1¼ ounces for a single shot or about 2 ounces for a double shot from a large filter. Both take about 20 seconds. Serve immediately.

Guide to Steaming and Foaming Milk

For the perfect steamed and foamed milk from your espresso maker, follow these guidelines:

☕ Always prepare steamed milk just before brewing the espresso, to ensure that your drink will be enjoyed at its hottest.

☕ Start with cold milk—whole, low-fat or nonfat. Pour it into a stainless-steel pitcher that will resist heat, yet let you feel the temperature—one-third full for foaming, two-thirds full for steaming. Insert a cooking thermometer into the pitcher, if you wish.

☕ Set your espresso machine to the steaming mode. Open the steam valve to clear any condensed water, then shut it.

☕ Holding the pitcher by its handle, place it under the steam jet.

☕ To foam milk: Position the tip of the jet just beneath the surface of the milk. Open the steam valve fully. Keep the tip of the jet barely beneath the surface, lowering the pitcher and incorporating more air as you foam.

☕ To steam milk: To heat milk without foaming, bury the nozzle near the bottom of the pitcher, taking care not to scald the milk. The ideal temperature is reached just when the side of your stainless-steel pitcher becomes too hot to touch for more than a second. A thermometer will register approximately 150°–170°F for steamed milk. Foamed milk, which incorporates air, will be a few degrees cooler.

☕ To avoid splattering, always turn off the steam valve before removing the pitcher.

☕ Immediately after use, wipe the jet clean with a damp cloth. With your hands safely clear, turn the steam valve on briefly to clear out any milk.

A Gallery of Espresso Drinks

Rich, intense espresso, a sublime experience on its own, becomes the foundation for
a wide variety of specialty drinks.

Espresso Macchiato (ess-PRESS-o mock-e-AH-toe) *Macchiato* **is Italian for "marked" or
"spotted," which describes the small dollop of milk foam added to a cup of espresso.**
Espresso—1 shot of espresso in a demitasse. *Foamed Milk*—Top with a dollop of foamed milk.

**Espresso con Panna (ess-PRESS-o cone PA-na) In this variation on a macchiato, a dollop of
whipped cream** *(panna)* **replaces the foamed milk.**
Espresso—1 shot of espresso in a demitasse. *Whipped Cream*—Top with a dollop of whipped cream.

Caffè Mocha (caf-AY MO-kah) A classic combination of espresso, chocolate and steamed milk.
Chocolate Syrup—Whatever size you make, pour in enough good-quality chocolate syrup to just
cover the bottom of the cup. *Espresso*—1 shot of espresso. *Steamed Milk*—Fill the cup almost to the
rim with steamed milk. *Whipped Cream*—Top with a dollop of whipped cream. *Cocoa Powder*—Lightly
sprinkle with cocoa powder.

Caffè Latte (caf-AY LAH-tay) The most popular morning coffee drink.
Espresso—1 shot of espresso. *Steamed Milk*—Fill the cup almost to the rim with steamed milk.
Foamed Milk—Top off with about ¼ inch of foamed milk.

**Cappuccino (cap-uh-CHEE-no) Named for the Catholic order of Capuchin friars, whose
hooded robes resemble the drink's cap of foam.**
Espresso—1 shot of espresso. *Steamed Milk*—Fill the cup halfway with steamed milk.
Foamed Milk—Top off above the rim with foamed milk.

**Caffè Americano (caf-AY a-mer-i-CAH-no) An Italian approach to typical American-strength
coffee, producing a full-flavored yet mild cup.**
Espresso—1 shot of espresso. *Water*—Fill with water just off the boil, 1 ounce short of the cup's capacity.

A Choice of Sizes

Espresso drinks may be made in a range of sizes, depending on how much you want to drink and on the
strength of coffee flavor you prefer.
Short. A basic 8-ounce cup, calling for 1 shot of espresso.
Tall. A 12-ounce cup or glass. Using 1 shot of espresso yields a milder coffee flavor than in a short; 2 shots yields
a stronger coffee presence, preferred by some people.
Grande. A 16-ounce cup or glass, calling for 2 shots of espresso and yielding drinks of the same strength as a short.

Recipes

Rhubarb Crumble

7 cups rhubarb (about 2 pounds total), cut into 1-inch pieces

⅓ cup granulated sugar

⅔ cup brown sugar, firmly packed

½ cup all-purpose flour

½ cup quick-cooking oatmeal

½ teaspoon ground cardamom or cinnamon

¼ teaspoon salt

6 tablespoons unsalted butter, cut into small pieces

Like a pie without a bottom crust, this old-fashioned recipe can be enjoyed any time of day. Complement the fruit's tartness with a syrupy varietal coffee such as Sumatra or a Sulawesi.

Preheat an oven to 425°F. In a large bowl, toss the rhubarb with the granulated sugar. Spread the rhubarb in an 8-inch-square baking pan, pressing it down lightly. Set aside.

In a medium bowl, combine the brown sugar, flour, oatmeal, cardamom or cinnamon, and salt. Add the butter and, with a pastry blender or your fingertips, blend it into the dry ingredients until the mixture is crumbly, with no visible lumps of butter.

Spread the topping evenly over the rhubarb. Bake for 15 minutes. Reduce the heat to 350°F and bake until the topping is browned and the rhubarb is tender when pierced with a thin, sharp knife, 20 minutes more. Serve warm or at room temperature.

Serves 4–6

Baked Apple-Almond Pudding

5 Golden Delicious,
   Cortland, McIntosh or
   Gravenstein apples
   (about 2 pounds total)

1 teaspoon vanilla extract

1 cup granulated sugar

2 eggs

¼ teaspoon almond
   extract

¼ teaspoon salt

1 cup all-purpose flour

½ cup unsalted butter,
   melted

½ cup finely chopped
   toasted almonds

Serve this home-style preparation either as a special brunch dish or at the end of a Sunday lunch or family dinner, matching the coffee to the occasion.

Preheat an oven to 325°F. Butter a 2-quart baking dish such as a round soufflé dish. Peel, halve and core the apples. Cut them into ½-inch cubes. Place the apples in a large bowl and toss with the vanilla and 2 tablespoons of the sugar. Spread the apples in the prepared dish.

In the same bowl, beat the remaining sugar with the eggs, almond extract and salt until blended. Add the flour and butter and beat until smooth. Stir in the almonds.

Spread the batter evenly over the fruit. Bake until the top is golden and the apples can be pierced easily with a thin, sharp knife, 50–60 minutes. Serve the pudding warm.

Serves 6

Grand City Granola

½ cup butter

¼ cup vegetable oil

1 cup honey

½ cup pure maple syrup

2 teaspoons salt

½ teaspoon ground cinnamon

½ teaspoon ground nutmeg

2 teaspoons vanilla extract

4 cups rolled oats

2⅔ cups barley flakes

1⅓ cups rye flakes

1⅓ cups wheat flakes

3½ cups nut pieces

⅔ cup coarsely shredded, unsweetened coconut

11 ounces dried fruit, cut into ⅜-inch pieces

1 cup dark raisins

For optimum taste and texture, use rolled oats, equal amounts of almond slices, walnuts, pecans and cashews for the nut pieces, and equal quantities of dates, prunes and apricots for the dried fruit. Enjoy with caffè latte or a bright Central American varietal.

Place the butter, vegetable oil, honey, maple syrup, salt, cinnamon, nutmeg and vanilla in a large saucepan over medium-low heat. Cook, stirring occasionally, until the butter is fully melted.

Preheat an oven to 300°F. In a large bowl, mix together the rolled oats, barley, rye and wheat flakes, nut pieces and coconut. Pour the warm butter mixture over the grains and toss with your hands or two large spoons until the grains are evenly coated.

Line a baking sheet with aluminum foil. Spread the grain mixture evenly over the foil and bake, turning the mixture every 10 minutes with a spoon or spatula, until the flakes begin to turn golden, 20–30 minutes. Be sure to turn all corners and surfaces so that the granola bakes evenly. The grains will seem a little sticky when done but will crisp as they cool.

Immediately after removing the granola from the oven, mix in the dried fruit and raisins and combine thoroughly. Let the granola cool completely and then store in an airtight container. It will keep for two weeks when stored in a cool place.

Makes about 4 pounds granola

Top to bottom: Apple Brown Betty (recipe page 50), Grand City Granola

Apple Brown Betty

3 cups fresh white bread crumbs (8–10 bread slices, including the crusts), lightly packed

½ cup unsalted butter, melted

6 Golden Delicious, Cortland, McIntosh or Gravenstein apples (about 2½ pounds total)

1 tablespoon lemon juice

⅔ cup granulated sugar

½ teaspoon ground cinnamon

¼ teaspoon ground nutmeg

¼ teaspoon salt

One of the most wholesome desserts, brown betty also makes a satisfying breakfast dish. Your favorite well-rounded coffee blend will suit it well.

Preheat an oven to 400°F. In a medium bowl, toss the bread crumbs with the melted butter. Set aside.

Peel, halve and core the apples. Cut them into thin slices; you should have about 7 cups. In a large bowl, toss the apples with the lemon juice, sugar, cinnamon, nutmeg and salt. Spread ½ cup of the crumbs over the bottom of a 2-quart baking dish such as a soufflé dish. Top with half of the sliced apples and sprinkle with another ½ cup of the crumbs. Spoon on the remaining apples and their juices, pressing the apples down lightly. Top with the remaining crumbs.

Butter a sheet of aluminum foil large enough to cover the baking dish. Place it, buttered side down, over the fruit and pinch around the edges to seal. Bake for 25 minutes, then remove the foil. Bake, uncovered, until the juices are bubbling, the crumbs are brown and the apples are tender when pierced with a thin, sharp knife, 30–40 minutes more. Serve warm or at room temperature.

Serves 4–6

Photograph page 49

Panettone

2 packages (5 teaspoons) active dry yeast

½ cup milk, warmed

4 cups all-purpose flour

¾ cup unsalted butter, at room temperature

1 teaspoon salt

¾ cup granulated sugar

4 eggs

4 egg yolks

¾ cup dark raisins

¾ cup golden raisins

½ cup finely chopped candied orange peel or citron

¼ cup grated orange zest

2 tablespoons grated lemon zest

Italy's classic egg-enriched fruit bread is traditionally baked in a special cylindrical mold. Instead, you can use two food cans 6 to 7 inches high and 5 inches wide. Serve with Italian roast or espresso.

In a small bowl, stir together the yeast and milk and let stand a few minutes.

In a large bowl, blend together the flour, butter and salt using a heavy-duty electric mixer or your fingertips. Add the sugar, eggs, egg yolks and dissolved yeast to the flour mixture and beat vigorously for about 2 minutes by machine or 4 minutes by hand. The batter should be stiff and heavy.

Add the dark and golden raisins, orange peel or citron, and orange and lemon zests. Beat vigorously to mix. Cover loosely and let rise until doubled in bulk, about 2 hours.

Generously butter two panettone molds. Beat the batter to deflate it. Divide it between the molds, filling them by less than half. Let rise until doubled in bulk, about 1 hour.

Preheat an oven to 375°F and place a rack in the lower level of the oven. Bake the panettone until puffy and browned, about 45 minutes. Cool 15 minutes, then remove from the molds and cool upright on a wire rack.

Makes 2 large loaves

Photograph page 52

Cinnamon-Swirl Biscuits

For the filling:

⅔ cup brown sugar, firmly packed

1½ teaspoons ground cinnamon

½ cup finely chopped walnuts

¼ cup dried currants or dark raisins

For the biscuits:

2 cups all-purpose flour

2 tablespoons granulated sugar

2 teaspoons baking powder

½ teaspoon baking soda

½ teaspoon salt

½ cup unsalted butter, at room temperature

⅔ cup buttermilk

3 tablespoons unsalted butter, melted

A quickly prepared cinnamon filling transforms easy buttermilk biscuit dough into sweet cinnamon rolls for the breakfast or brunch table. Enjoy them with your favorite morning coffee.

Preheat an oven to 425°F. Butter two 8-inch-diameter cake pans.

To make the filling, in a small bowl, mix together the brown sugar, cinnamon, walnuts and currants or raisins. Set aside.

To make the biscuits, sift the flour, granulated sugar, baking powder, baking soda and salt into a large bowl. Add the ½ cup butter and, with a pastry blender or your fingertips, blend it into the dry ingredients until the mixture resembles fine, irregular crumbs. Add the buttermilk and stir until the dough forms a cohesive mass.

Turn the dough onto a floured work surface and knead gently about 10 times. Push and pat the dough into a rectangle about 12 inches long and 4 inches wide. Brush with the 3 tablespoons butter. Spread the filling over the dough and press it in gently. Starting at one of the long sides of the rectangle, roll the dough into a tight cylinder. Using a sharp knife, cut the roll into slices about 1 inch thick.

Place the slices, cut side down and about ½ inch apart, in the prepared pans. Bake until the biscuits are puffy and lightly browned, about 15 minutes. Serve warm.

Makes about 1 dozen biscuits

Left to right: Cinnamon-Swirl Biscuits, Panettone (recipe page 51)

Apricot-Citrus Scones

For the scones:

3 cups all-purpose flour

½ cup granulated sugar

2½ teaspoons baking powder

1 teaspoon salt

½ teaspoon baking soda

¾ cup unsalted butter, at room temperature

2 tablespoons grated orange zest

about ¾ cup finely diced dried apricots

½ cup chopped pecans

1 cup buttermilk

For the glaze:

2 tablespoons heavy cream

2 teaspoons granulated sugar

Use soft, moist dried apricots. If yours are firm and chewy, soak them for 15 minutes in boiling water and drain well. As a counterpoint to the tartness of the dried fruit, choose a full-bodied Indonesian coffee.

Preheat an oven to 425°F and butter a baking sheet. In a large bowl, mix together the flour, sugar, baking powder, salt and baking soda. Blend the butter into the dry ingredients, using your fingertips or a pastry blender, until the mixture is crumbly. Add the orange zest, apricots and pecans and toss to combine. Add the buttermilk and stir until the dough is rough and shaggy.

Gather the dough together and place on a generously floured work surface. Knead gently about 10 times. Divide the dough in half and pat each piece into a circle about 7 inches in diameter and ½ inch thick. To glaze, brush the circles with the cream and sprinkle with the sugar. Cut each round into eight pie-shaped wedges. Place the scones, barely touching, on the prepared baking sheet. Bake until puffy and golden, 15–18 minutes.

Makes 16 scones

Blueberry Coffee Cake

For the topping:

½ cup all-purpose flour

¼ cup granulated sugar

½ teaspoon ground cinnamon

2 tablespoons unsalted butter

For the cake:

1 egg

1 cup milk

¼ cup unsalted butter, melted

2 cups all-purpose flour

½ cup granulated sugar

2½ teaspoons baking powder

½ teaspoon salt

½ teaspoon ground mace

1 cup fresh or frozen blueberries

Try substituting raspberries for the blueberries in this flavorful morning coffee cake.

Preheat an oven to 350°F. Butter a 9-inch-diameter cake pan. To make the topping, in a small bowl, combine the flour, sugar and cinnamon. Blend in the butter, using your fingertips or a pastry blender, until the mixture is crumbly. Set aside.

To make the cake, in a large bowl, beat together the egg, milk and butter. Sift the flour, sugar, baking powder, salt and mace into a small bowl and add to the egg mixture. Beat until just blended. Gently stir in the blueberries.

Spread the batter evenly in the prepared pan and sprinkle with the topping. Bake until a wood toothpick inserted in the center of the cake comes out clean, 40–45 minutes. Serve warm from the pan.

Serves 6–8

Peach Kuchen with Crumble Topping

For the kuchen:

3–4 very ripe, large peaches (about 2 pounds total), blanched for 10 seconds and the skins removed, or 1 pound frozen peach slices, thawed

2 tablespoons lemon juice

1½ cups sifted all-purpose flour

2 teaspoons baking powder

½ teaspoon salt

½ cup granulated sugar

2 extra-large eggs

2 tablespoons milk

grated zest of 1 lemon

½ cup unsalted butter, melted

For the topping:

⅓ cup dark brown sugar, firmly packed

½ teaspoon ground cinnamon

½ teaspoon ground ginger

For the glaze:

1 extra-large egg yolk

¼ cup heavy cream

1 rounded tablespoon light brown sugar

A simple topping and a glaze, added at different stages of baking, enliven a homey coffee cake filled with fresh summer fruit. Serve with your favorite varietal, blend or espresso drink.

Preheat an oven to 375°F. Butter and flour a 9-inch springform pan.

To make the kuchen, cut the ripe peaches into slices. Place the fresh or thawed peach slices in a bowl and sprinkle with the lemon juice. Set aside. Resift the flour with the baking powder, salt and sugar into a medium bowl. In a small bowl, beat the eggs and milk. Stir in the lemon zest. Dribble this mixture over the flour, then stir in the butter. Mix only until the ingredients are incorporated. Spread the batter in the bottom of the prepared pan. Drain the peaches and arrange the slices on top of the batter.

To make the topping, combine all the ingredients in a small bowl. Sprinkle the topping on the batter. Bake the kuchen for 25 minutes.

Meanwhile, to make the glaze, thoroughly mix all the ingredients in a small bowl. Pour the glaze over the kuchen and bake until the top has set, 10–15 minutes more.

Cool the kuchen in the pan for 15 minutes. Release the springform and cut the kuchen into servings.

Serves 8

Hazelnut–Raspberry Muffins

3 cups sifted all-purpose flour

4 teaspoons baking powder

¼ teaspoon baking soda

1 teaspoon salt

⅔ cup dark brown sugar, firmly packed

about 3½ ounces hazelnuts, lightly toasted and coarsely chopped

⅔ cup orange juice

1 extra-large egg, slightly beaten

⅔ cup milk

½ cup unsalted butter, melted

grated zest of 1 orange

1¼ cups fresh raspberries or frozen raspberries, thawed and drained

Combining tangy fruit and rich nuts, these muffins go well with a coffee that exhibits similar tastes: the walnutty Colombia Nariño Supremo, for example, or the berrylike Ethiopia Harrar.

Preheat an oven to 350°F. Generously butter standard muffin tins.

In a large bowl, resift the flour with the baking powder, baking soda and salt. Stir in the sugar and hazelnuts and toss until the nuts are lightly coated with flour. In a medium bowl, combine the orange juice, egg, milk, butter and orange zest. Stir into the dry ingredients just until incorporated. Gently stir in the raspberries.

Divide the batter among the muffin tins. Bake until golden brown, about 20 minutes. If the muffins brown too quickly before the centers are done, lower the oven temperature to 375°F. Transfer the muffins from the pan to a wire rack to cool.

Makes about 20 muffins

Pear-Ginger Muffins

4 ounces dried pears

1 ripe Bosc, Bartlett or Anjou pear

2 cups all-purpose flour

2 teaspoons baking powder

½ teaspoon baking soda

½ teaspoon salt

½ teaspoon ground nutmeg

2 eggs

⅔ cup granulated sugar

½ cup milk

1 teaspoon vanilla extract

⅓ cup unsalted butter, melted

⅓ cup finely chopped candied ginger

Dried and fresh pears add rich texture, intense flavor and moist tenderness to these breakfast treats. Enjoy them with a cappuccino, a caffè latte or your favorite morning blend.

In a small bowl, cover the dried pears with boiling water and let stand 15 minutes. Preheat an oven to 400°F and butter standard muffin tins.

Drain the pears well and pat them dry with paper towels. With scissors or a sharp knife, cut the pears into ½-inch pieces. Peel, core and finely dice the ripe pear. In a medium bowl, stir and toss together the flour, baking powder, baking soda, salt and nutmeg. In a small bowl, whisk together the eggs, sugar, milk, vanilla, butter, ginger and fresh and dried pears. Add to the dry ingredients and stir just until the batter is blended.

Spoon the batter into the prepared muffin tins, filling each cup about two-thirds full. Bake until a wood toothpick inserted in the center of a muffin comes out clean, 15–18 minutes. Cool for 5 minutes, then remove from the pan.

Makes 1 dozen muffins

Streusel-Crumb Coffee Cake

For the streusel:

1½ cups graham cracker crumbs

¾ cup finely chopped walnuts

¾ cup brown sugar, firmly packed

1 teaspoon ground cinnamon

¼ teaspoon ground cardamom

½ cup unsalted butter, melted

For the cake:

2 cups cake flour

1 cup granulated sugar

2½ teaspoons baking powder

½ teaspoon salt

½ cup unsalted butter, at room temperature

2 eggs

1½ teaspoons vanilla extract

1 cup milk

Crushed graham crackers and chopped walnuts give extra distinction to the crunchy, sweetly spiced streusel topping of this classic morning coffee cake.

Preheat an oven to 350°F. Butter and flour a 10-inch tube pan, a 9-inch springform pan or an 8-inch-square baking pan.

To make the streusel, in a medium bowl, combine the graham cracker crumbs, walnuts, brown sugar, cinnamon, cardamom and melted butter. Blend well and set aside.

To make the cake, sift the flour, sugar, baking powder and salt into a large bowl. Add the butter, eggs, vanilla and milk. Beat vigorously until smooth and quite thick, about 1 minute.

Spread half of the batter in the prepared pan and sprinkle with half of the streusel mixture. Spoon the remaining batter over the streusel, then top with the remaining streusel. Bake until a wood toothpick inserted in the center of the cake comes out clean, about 50 minutes. Cool about 20 minutes, then remove the cake from the pan.

Serves 10–12

Financiers

1 cup sliced almonds, toasted

1 ¼ cups confectioners' sugar

½ cup all-purpose flour

3 egg whites

¼ teaspoon salt

¼ teaspoon almond extract

2 tablespoons granulated sugar

½ cup unsalted butter, melted

35–40 whole almonds

Ground almonds and beaten egg whites make these little afternoon or after-dinner cakes reminiscent of Italian amaretti, at once rich—as the name implies—and light. They're especially good with espresso.

Preheat an oven to 375°F. Generously butter miniature muffin tins (with cups that hold 2 tablespoons) or madeleine pans, or coat them with nonstick cooking spray.

Grind the almonds finely in a food processor or blender; set aside. Sift the confectioners' sugar and flour together onto waxed paper; set aside. In a large bowl, beat the egg whites, salt and almond extract until the whites are foamy and droopy. Add the granulated sugar and beat until soft peaks form. Sift the confectioners' sugar mixture over the egg whites and add the ground almonds. Fold the dry ingredients into the egg whites until blended. Gently stir in the butter.

Spoon about 1 tablespoon of the batter into each mold and place a whole almond on top. Bake until the cakes are dry on top and lightly browned around the edges, 10–12 minutes. (If using standard muffin tins, fill them with about 2 tablespoons batter; bake 15–18 minutes.) Gently lift the cakes to a wire rack to cool completely.

Makes about 3 dozen miniature cakes or 1½ dozen large cakes

Top to bottom: Financiers, Classic Lemon Sponge Cake (recipe page 64)

Classic Lemon Sponge Cake

6 extra-large eggs, at room temperature

1 cup granulated sugar

2 tablespoons lemon juice

grated zest of 1 large lemon

1 cup cake flour, sifted

½ teaspoon salt

confectioners' sugar, for dusting

This light, pleasing cake is especially good with vanilla ice cream or raspberry sauce. The hint of berries in Ethiopia Harrar or the hint of black currant in Kenya coffee complements the cake nicely.

Preheat an oven to 325°F and place a rack in the lower third of the oven, but not in the lowest position. Butter the bottom, but not the sides, of a 10-inch tube pan with a removable bottom. Cut a piece of parchment paper to fit the bottom, set it in place, lightly butter it and then dust it with flour.

In a large bowl, place the eggs and sugar and, with an electric mixer, beat at high speed until the mixture is very thick, 10–15 minutes. A heavy, light yellow ribbon should form when the beaters are lifted from the bowl. Add the lemon juice and zest and continue mixing for 3 more minutes.

Resift ½ cup of the flour with ¼ teaspoon of the salt over the egg-sugar mixture and, using a rubber spatula, fold in gently. Repeat with the remaining flour and salt. Make sure no traces of flour remain, being careful not to overwork the batter.

Pour the batter into the prepared pan, smoothing the top with a rubber spatula. Bake until a wood toothpick inserted in the center comes out clean, about 50 minutes.

Invert the cake pan on top of a wire rack to cool. When the cake has cooled to room temperature, remove the sides of the pan. Invert the cake onto a flat plate and discard the parchment paper. Sift the confectioners' sugar over the top.

Serves 8–10

Photograph page 63

Orange-Pecan Pound Cake

2 cups all-purpose flour

½ teaspoon salt

1 cup unsalted butter, at
    room temperature

1 teaspoon vanilla extract

¼ cup grated orange zest

1⅔ cups granulated sugar

5 eggs, at room
    temperature

¼ cup bourbon

¼ cup milk

½ cup chopped pecans

If you like, try lightly toasting slices of this fragrant cake before

serving with a caffè latte or cappuccino.

Preheat an oven to 350°F. Butter and flour a 10-inch tube pan or
bundt pan, or two 8½- by 4½- by 2½-inch loaf pans.

Sift together the flour and salt onto a piece of waxed paper. In a
large bowl, beat the butter, vanilla and orange zest until smooth.
Continue to beat while adding the sugar, then beat until blended.
Add the eggs, one at a time, beating well after each addition,
then beat until light and fluffy. Add the bourbon, milk and about
half of the flour to the egg mixture and beat to blend. Add the
remaining flour and beat until smooth. Stir in the pecans.

Spread the batter evenly in the prepared pan or pans. Bake
until a wood toothpick inserted in the center of the cake comes
out clean, about 60 minutes for a tube or bundt pan, about 45
minutes for loaf pans. Cool 10 minutes, then turn the cake
onto a wire rack to cool completely.

Serves 12–16

Photograph page 66

Top to bottom: Raisin Gingerbread with Ginger Icing,
Orange-Pecan Pound Cake (recipe page 65)

Raisin Gingerbread with Ginger Icing

For the gingerbread:

⅔ cup dark brown sugar, firmly packed

⅔ cup molasses

⅔ cup boiling water

¼ cup unsalted butter, at room temperature, cut into chunks

1 teaspoon baking soda

1 extra-large egg, well beaten

½ cup dark raisins

1½ cups all-purpose flour, sifted

1 teaspoon ground cinnamon

1 teaspoon ground ginger

¼ teaspoon ground cloves

¼ cup finely chopped candied ginger

For the icing:

¼ cup unsalted butter, at room temperature

¼ pound cream cheese, at room temperature

1½ cups confectioners' sugar, sifted

1 teaspoon vanilla extract

¼ cup finely chopped candied ginger

Try highlighting old-fashioned gingerbread by serving it with a varietal that offers hints of spice—such as Arabian Mocha Sanani or Guatemala Antigua—or with a sweet and spicy espresso roast.

Preheat an oven to 350°F. Butter and flour a 9-inch-square baking pan.

To make the gingerbread, in a large bowl, combine the brown sugar, molasses, boiling water and butter. Blend together by hand or with an electric mixer set on low. While the mixture is still hot, add the baking soda, egg and raisins.

In a small bowl, resift the flour with the cinnamon, ginger and cloves. Stir into the molasses mixture. Add the candied ginger and mix well without incorporating too many air bubbles.

Pour the batter into the prepared pan. Bake until a wood tooth-pick inserted in the center comes out clean, 35–40 minutes. Cool the gingerbread completely.

To make the icing, in a small bowl, beat together the butter and cream cheese until smooth. Add the sugar and beat until smooth. Mix in the vanilla and candied ginger. Chill briefly before frosting the gingerbread.

Serves 8

Butterscotch Ranger Cookies

1 cup unsalted butter, at room temperature

1 cup granulated sugar

1 cup brown sugar, firmly packed

2 eggs

2 teaspoons vanilla extract

1 tablespoon water

2 cups all-purpose flour

1 teaspoon baking soda

½ teaspoon baking powder

½ teaspoon salt

2 cups regular or quick-cooking oatmeal

2 cups butterscotch morsels

2 cups cornflakes

1 cup chopped walnuts (optional)

There's something wild, rugged and just plain fun about this chewy combination of oats, cornflakes and butterscotch chips. A well-rounded coffee blend goes just right with them.

Preheat an oven to 350°F. Butter one or two cookie sheets, or coat them with nonstick cooking spray.

In a large bowl, beat the butter and granulated and brown sugars until mixed. Beat in the eggs, one at a time. Then beat in the vanilla and the water. In a medium bowl, toss together the flour, baking soda, baking powder and salt. Add the dry ingredients to the butter mixture and beat until combined. Add the oatmeal, butterscotch morsels, cornflakes and walnuts (if using) and mix well.

Place heaping teaspoonfuls of batter, about 2 inches apart, onto the prepared baking sheets. With moistened fingertips, gently press each cookie to flatten it slightly. Bake the cookies until lightly browned, about 12 minutes. Transfer to wire racks to cool completely.

Makes about 80 cookies

Brandied Walnut-Prune Cake

3½ cups cake flour

4 teaspoons baking powder

1 teaspoon salt

1 teaspoon ground mace or ground nutmeg

1 cup unsalted butter, at room temperature

2 cups granulated sugar

2 teaspoons vanilla extract

6 eggs, at room temperature

½ cup brandy, Cognac, bourbon or other whiskey

½ cup milk

3 cups walnuts, in halves or large pieces

3 cups coarsely chopped pitted prunes

Dense with fruit and nuts and aromatic with brandy, thin slices of this cake make a satisfying accompaniment to afternoon or after-dinner coffee.

Preheat an oven to 325°F. Butter and flour a 10-inch tube pan or bundt pan.

Sift the cake flour, baking powder, salt and mace or nutmeg onto a sheet of waxed paper. In a large bowl, beat the butter and sugar until blended. Beat in the vanilla. Add the eggs, one at a time, beating well after each addition. In a small bowl, stir together the brandy and milk and add to the egg mixture along with the dry ingredients. Beat until the batter is blended and smooth. Stir in the walnuts and prunes.

Spread the batter evenly in the prepared pan and bake until a thin wood skewer inserted in the center of the cake comes out clean, or with just a few moist crumbs attached, 60–70 minutes. Cool 10 minutes, then turn the cake onto a wire rack to cool completely.

Serves 12–16

Chocolate Fudge Squares with Mocha Glaze

For the squares:

½ cup unsalted butter, at room temperature

1 cup granulated sugar

1 extra-large egg

1 cup all-purpose flour

¼ teaspoon baking powder

2 ounces unsweetened chocolate, melted

½ cup milk

1 teaspoon vanilla extract

½ cup chopped walnuts

For the glaze:

1 generous cup confectioners' sugar

1 tablespoon unsalted butter, at room temperature

1 ounce unsweetened chocolate, melted

1 teaspoon vanilla extract

¼ cup double-strength coffee, brewed from freshly ground beans

Beating by hand ensures a rich, creamy texture for these confections. Virtually any varietal or blend of coffee complements their intense chocolate flavor.

Preheat an oven to 350°F. Butter an 8-inch-square baking pan.

To make the squares, in a large bowl, cream the butter with the sugar and egg. In a small bowl, sift together the flour and baking powder. Add to the butter mixture. Then add the melted chocolate, being careful not to overbeat. Add the milk, vanilla and walnuts, stirring just to blend. Pour the batter into the prepared pan. Bake until the edges begin to pull away from the sides of the pan and the top springs back when pressed lightly, about 30 minutes. Allow the cake to cool completely.

Meanwhile, to make the glaze, in a medium bowl, combine the sugar, butter, chocolate and vanilla. Stir in the coffee and whisk until smooth. Refrigerate the glaze until cool, then pour over the top of the cake and cut the cake into squares.

Makes 16 squares

Almond Macaroons

8 ounces almond paste

½ cup granulated sugar

¼ cup confectioners' sugar

½ teaspoon almond extract

¼ teaspoon salt

2 or 3 egg whites (⅓ cup total)

Light and crisp, these classic macaroons practically melt in the mouth. See if you can resist dipping them, only briefly, into a cup of espresso or black coffee.

Preheat an oven to 350°F. Cover two baking sheets with parchment paper.

Break the almond paste into pieces and drop the pieces in a food processor. Process until broken into powdery bits. Add the granulated sugar, confectioners' sugar, almond extract and salt and process for about 1 minute. Add the egg whites and process just until blended and smooth. Alternatively, place the almond paste, sugars, almond extract and salt in a large bowl and work the ingredients together with your fingers. Add the egg whites and stir vigorously until blended. The mixture will be quite soft but not runny, about the consistency of a thick batter.

Drop generous teaspoonfuls of batter, about 2 inches apart, onto the prepared baking sheets. With moistened fingertips, gently smooth the surface of each macaroon. Bake until the macaroons are golden and crusty on top, 25–30 minutes. Let the macaroons cool completely on the baking sheets. When cold, turn the parchment paper, with the macaroons attached, upside down. Dampen the back of the paper with a wet towel, wait a moment and peel the macaroons away from the paper.

Makes about 25 macaroons

Coffee Frappé

18–22 ice cubes, crushed

7 fluid ounces double-strength coffee, chilled

2 tablespoons granulated sugar

2 tablespoons vanilla, hazelnut, raspberry or other syrup

whipped cream or ice cream, for garnish

Refreshingly icy, this coffee drink tastes especially good made with a well-balanced blend of varietals such as the combination of East African and Arabian coffees used in Gazebo Blend®.

Place the ice, coffee, sugar and syrup in a blender. Blend until the frappé is smooth. Pour into a large, tall glass. Garnish with a dollop of whipped cream or a scoop of your favorite ice cream.

Makes one 16-ounce frappé

Mocha Frappé

18–22 ice cubes, crushed

7 fluid ounces double-strength coffee, chilled

¼ cup chocolate sauce

2 tablespoons vanilla, almond, raspberry or other syrup

whipped cream or ice cream, for garnish

Yemeni coffees shipped from the old port of Al Mukah had such a chocolaty taste that the port's name gave rise to the word *mocha* to refer to a mixture of coffee and chocolate. Try making this with the classic Mocha Java blend.

Place the ice, coffee, chocolate sauce and syrup in a blender. Blend until the frappé is smooth. Pour into a large, tall glass. Garnish with a dollop of whipped cream or a scoop of your favorite ice cream.

Makes one 16-ounce frappé

Left to right: Mocha Frappé, Coffee Frappé

Lemon-Tipped Pistachio Biscotti

For the biscotti:

6 tablespoons unsalted butter, at room temperature

½ cup granulated sugar

1 tablespoon grated lemon zest

2 large eggs

1 teaspoon vanilla extract

2 cups all-purpose flour

2 teaspoons baking powder

¼ teaspoon salt

1 cup shelled pistachios, roasted and coarsely chopped

For the lemon icing:

2 cups sifted confectioners' sugar

1 teaspoon grated lemon zest

¼ cup lemon juice

Zesty icing adds elegance to Italy's signature cookie, which can be enjoyed any time of day.

Preheat an oven to 375°F. In a large bowl, beat the butter, sugar and lemon zest until well blended. Add the eggs, one at a time, beating well after each addition. Stir in the vanilla. In a small bowl, combine the flour, baking powder and salt. Add to the butter mixture and blend thoroughly. Stir in the nuts. The dough will be soft.

On a lightly floured work surface, divide the dough in half. Lightly flour each piece and shape it into a log about 1½ inches in diameter and 9 inches long. Place the logs about 3 inches apart on an ungreased baking sheet. Press each log down to make it about ¾ inch thick and 3 inches wide. Bake until puffed and lightly browned on top, about 20 minutes. Cool 10 minutes on the pan, then slide the logs onto a work surface. Using a long, sharp knife, cut each log crosswise into ¾-inch-thick slices. Make each cut with a single swipe of the blade. Don't use a sawing motion, which will break the cookies.

Place the cookies, cut side down, on the baking sheet. (The cookies can be touching.) Bake 10 minutes. Remove from the oven and, using tongs, turn each cookie over. Bake until the biscotti are golden, 10 minutes more. Transfer to wire racks to cool completely.

To make the icing, in a small bowl, combine the sugar, lemon zest and lemon juice and beat until smooth. Beat in additional drops of lemon juice if necessary to make an icing that will coat the biscotti lightly. Dip one end of each biscotti in the icing, turning to coat the tip evenly. Place on a wire rack until the icing sets.

Makes about 2½ dozen biscotti

Left to right: Lemon-Tipped Pistachio Biscotti, Chocolate-Hazelnut Biscotti (recipe page 78)

Chocolate-Hazelnut Biscotti

½ cup unsalted butter, at room temperature

¾ cup granulated sugar

1 tablespoon grated orange zest

3 large eggs

1 teaspoon vanilla extract

3 cups all-purpose flour

1 tablespoon baking powder

½ teaspoon salt

1 cup hazelnuts, lightly toasted and coarsely chopped

8 ounces semisweet chocolate chips, melted

These twice-baked Italian cookies are perfect for dipping in espresso.

Preheat an oven to 350°F. In a large bowl, beat together the butter, sugar and orange zest. Add the eggs, one at a time, beating well after each addition. Stir in the vanilla. In a small bowl, combine the flour, baking powder and salt. Add to the butter mixture and stir to blend thoroughly. Stir in the nuts. The dough will be soft.

On a lightly floured work surface, divide the dough into three equal pieces. Lightly flour each piece and shape it into a log about 1½ inches in diameter and 8–9 inches long. Place the logs about 3 inches apart on an ungreased baking sheet. Press each log down to make it about ¾ inch thick and 3 inches wide. Bake until puffed and lightly browned on top, about 20 minutes. Cool 10 minutes on the pan, then slide the logs onto a work surface. Using a long, sharp knife, cut each log crosswise into ¾-inch-thick slices. Make each cut with a single swipe of the blade. Don't use a sawing motion, which will break the cookies.

Place the cookies, cut side down, on the baking sheet. (The cookies can be touching.) Bake 10 minutes. Remove from the oven and, using tongs, turn each cookie over. Bake until the biscotti are lightly browned, 10–14 minutes more. Transfer to wire racks to cool completely.

Place about 1 teaspoon of melted chocolate on the tip of each biscotti and spread the chocolate from the tip to the center so the biscotti is nearly half-covered. Place the biscotti on a wire rack and let set until the chocolate is hard, 2–3 hours.

Makes about 3½ dozen biscotti

Photograph page 77

pastry for Caramel-Honey Nut Tartlets (see recipe on page 91; follow instructions for making the pastry)

1 cup milk

¼ cup granulated sugar

4 teaspoons cornstarch

pinch of salt

3 egg yolks

1 tablespoon unsalted butter

1 teaspoon vanilla extract

½ cup red currant jelly

2 teaspoons lemon juice

1½ cups fresh blueberries, stems removed

1½ cups fresh raspberries, stems removed

Fresh Berry Cream Tartlets

Serve these luscious tartlets with your favorite dark-roast blend.

Preheat an oven to 425°F. Divide the pastry into four equal pieces. Pat each piece evenly over the bottom and sides of a 4½-inch-diameter tartlet pan with a removable bottom. To keep the pastry from becoming misshapen while baking, press a square of aluminum foil snugly into each pastry shell. Bake for 12 minutes. Lift off the foil and bake until golden and crisp, 3–4 minutes. If the pastry puffs, prick it with a fork. Cool before filling.

Heat the milk in a small saucepan. Meanwhile, blend the sugar, cornstarch and salt in a small bowl. Whisk in the hot milk. Return the mixture to the saucepan and cook over medium heat, whisking constantly, until it boils and thickens, about 5 minutes. Remove from the heat, add the egg yolks and whisk until smooth. Return to the heat and cook, whisking constantly, about 2 minutes more. Stir in the butter. Cool until tepid, stirring frequently, then add the vanilla. Cover and refrigerate the custard if you are not assembling the tartlets immediately.

To make the glaze, combine the jelly and lemon juice in a small pan and bring to a boil, stirring to blend. Cool a few minutes, then brush a thin coat of glaze over the inside of the pastry shells. Let set a moment. Stir the custard vigorously, then spread it evenly in the pastry shells.

Arrange the berries, stem end down, in concentric circles over the custard. Mound extra berries in the center. Brush the remaining glaze lightly over the berries (reheat the glaze if it has jelled). Refrigerate the tarts if not serving immediately. Remove from the refrigerator about 30 minutes before serving.

Serves 4

Photograph page 45

The World's Best Chocolate Pudding

4 extra-large egg yolks

¾ cup granulated sugar

¼ cup all-purpose flour

3 tablespoons cornstarch

2½ cups milk

5 ounces semisweet
chocolate, finely
chopped

2 ounces unsweetened
chocolate, finely
chopped

1 teaspoon vanilla extract

4 ounces white chocolate,
cut into ½-inch pieces

whipped cream, for serving

This may sound like a grand claim. But three kinds of chocolate give this pudding intense flavor and richness. Your favorite varietal or blend, whatever it might be, makes the perfect companion.

In a medium bowl, mix the egg yolks, sugar, flour and cornstarch. Add 1 or 2 tablespoons of the milk and mix to make a smooth paste.

In a medium saucepan over medium-high heat, scald the remaining milk. Remove from the heat and stir into the egg-flour mixture. Pour the milk-flour mixture back into the saucepan and place over medium heat, whisking constantly until it begins to boil and thicken. Reduce the heat to low and cook for 2 more minutes, stirring constantly. Take care not to let the bottom burn. Remove the saucepan from the heat and add the semisweet and unsweetened chocolates and vanilla. Stir until the chocolate melts and the mixture is smooth. Let cool for 5 minutes, then gently fold in the white chocolate pieces just to incorporate.

Spoon the pudding into individual glasses. Cool at room temperature, then refrigerate until serving time. Garnish each serving with a dollop of whipped cream.

Serves 6–8

Pear and Honey Clafoutis

2–3 Bartlett, Anjou or
  Comice pears (about
  1 pound total)

juice of 1 lime

4 extra-large eggs

⅓ cup granulated sugar

2 tablespoons unsalted
  butter, melted

1 cup heavy cream

1 teaspoon ground ginger
  or 1 tablespoon
  chopped candied
  ginger (optional)

finely julienned zest of 1
  lime

⅓ cup honey

Serve this rustic Provençal tart warm or cool, plain or with vanilla ice cream. To go with it, try brewing a rich, varietal such as Sumatra or Sulawesi, or your favorite full-bodied blend.

Preheat an oven to 350°F. Generously butter a 9-inch-diameter glass or ceramic quiche pan. Place the pan on a heavy-duty baking sheet lined with aluminum foil (to protect the oven in case of spills).

Peel and core the pears and cut them into thin slices. Place the slices in a small bowl, add the lime juice and toss. In a medium bowl, whisk together the eggs, sugar, butter and cream. Stir in the ginger (if using) and the lime zest.

Pour a thin layer of the egg mixture into the quiche pan. Drain the pear slices and layer them over the egg mixture. Pour in the remaining egg mixture. Dribble the honey over the top. Bake until the top is puffed and browned and the filling is set, 25–30 minutes. Serve the clafoutis warm.

Serves 6–8

Baked Apples Stuffed with Mascarpone

4 large Cortland, Rome or McIntosh apples (about 2 pounds total)

¼ cup dried currants

⅓ cup brandy

6 ounces mascarpone

½ cup chopped walnuts

½ cup dark brown sugar, firmly packed

Mascarpone, a tangy, almost-liquid Italian cream cheese, adds distinction to homey baked apples. Try serving this with a sturdy, sweet Italian roast or with a syrupy, earthy Indonesian varietal.

Preheat an oven to 350°F. Core the apples, leaving the bottoms intact. Peel off the skin around the top, leaving two-thirds of the apple unpeeled. Use a grapefruit spoon to hollow out about a 1½-inch-wide by 2½-inch-deep pocket in the center of each apple.

Place the currants and brandy in a small saucepan over low heat. Bring to a simmer and remove from the heat. Pour the currants and brandy into a small bowl and let cool. When cool, mix in the mascarpone, walnuts and brown sugar. Fill the pockets of the apples with the stuffing and place the apples in a shallow baking pan. Add about 1 inch of water. Bake until the apples are tender, about 30 minutes. Serve the stuffed apples warm or cold.

Serves 4

Coffee Crème Brûlée

For the custard:

5½ cups heavy cream

¼ cup very coarsely
    ground espresso beans

8 extra-large egg yolks

⅔ cup granulated sugar

For the topping:

2–3 tablespoons boiling
    water

1⅓ cups dark brown
    sugar, firmly packed

For serving:

edible gold-leaf stars

Espresso enlivens this version of the caramel-crusted French custard.

Preheat an oven to 350°F and place a rack in the lower third of the oven. Set eight 8-ounce custard cups or ramekins in a shallow roasting pan or jelly-roll pan with at least 1-inch-high sides. The cups should not touch each other.

To make the custard, in a medium saucepan over medium heat, heat the cream and ground espresso beans until small bubbles form around the rim. Strain the cream through a fine sieve to remove the coffee. In a medium metal bowl, combine the egg yolks and granulated sugar and whisk for 1 minute. Whisk a little of the hot espresso cream into the yolk mixture and then add the remaining espresso cream.

Divide the mixture among the eight custard cups. Place the pan with the cups into the oven and add to the pan about ½ inch of boiling water. Bake until the custards are set, about 40 minutes. Remove the custards from the water. Cool at room temperature for 20 minutes and then refrigerate until cold.

To make the topping, preheat a broiler and place the broiler rack in the top position, about 3 inches below the heating element. In a small bowl, combine the boiling water and brown sugar to make a thick paste. Using the back of a teaspoon, spread 1–2 tablespoons of the topping on each custard, covering the top all the way to the sides of the cup.

Set the cups on a heavy-duty baking sheet and place under the broiler until the sugar bubbles and just begins to get very brown, 2–3 minutes. If you can smell the sugar burning, it is time to remove the cups from the oven. Let the custards cool, then refrigerate at least 15 minutes before serving. Garnish each serving with gold-leaf stars.

Serves 8

Nut Lace Cookies

¼ cup unsalted butter

¼ cup light corn syrup

¼ cup brown sugar, firmly packed

¼ cup all-purpose flour

pinch of salt

1 cup coarsely chopped or broken nuts, one kind or a mixture (almonds, hazelnuts, pecans, macadamias, pine nuts, pistachios, walnuts)

Reminiscent of Florentines, but without a chocolate coating, these light confections go delightfully with a mild blend or a delicate varietal such as Kona or Mexico Altura.

Preheat an oven to 350°F. Coat a large, sturdy baking sheet with nonstick cooking spray. In a large saucepan over low heat, melt the butter. Add the corn syrup and brown sugar. Increase the heat to high and stir the mixture until it boils. Remove the pan from the heat and add the flour, salt and nuts. Beat until blended. The batter will be stiff and sticky.

For each cookie, place 2 tablespoons of the nut mixture on the prepared baking sheet, spacing the cookies 6–7 inches apart. A large baking sheet will hold four cookies; a smaller sheet will hold two or three. With moistened fingertips, pat each cookie into a 3-inch circle. Ignore holes or gaps in the circles; most of them will disappear in baking. Bake until the cookies have spread and are a rich golden brown, 8–10 minutes. Let the cookies cool on the pan until they are still malleable but are firm enough to remove with a spatula, 2–2½ minutes.

Carefully transfer the cookies to a wire rack to cool and crisp. (If the cookies become hard and stick to the pan, return them to the oven for a moment to soften.) Bake the remaining batter. Wipe the pan with paper towels and coat it lightly with nonstick spray between each batch. The cookies break easily, so store them in a sturdy, airtight container and place waxed paper between the cookies to protect them.

Makes 1 dozen cookies

Top to bottom: Chocolate-Dipped Fruit (recipe page 88), Nut Lace Cookies

Chocolate-Dipped Fruit

6 ounces semisweet
chocolate

2 ounces unsweetened
chocolate

6–8 ounces dried apricots,
figs, pineapples or
pears, or about
20 medium-sized fresh
strawberries, rinsed
and thoroughly dried

Present a selection of these simply prepared, elegant treats with

espresso or your favorite after-dinner coffee. You can also dip

Candied Citrus Peel (page 94) in the same way.

Chop the chocolates coarsely. Combine them in a medium bowl and melt partially, either over simmering water or in a microwave. When the chocolate is about half-melted, remove from the heat and whisk vigorously until completely smooth. To maintain the proper consistency, set the bowl of chocolate in a larger bowl of hot tap water. Replace the water as it cools, taking care not to splash the water into the chocolate.

Spear each piece of fruit with a wood toothpick. Dip it in the chocolate and turn it to coat completely. If you wish, dip some fruit halfway so they are only partially covered in chocolate. Nudge the fruit from the toothpick onto a piece of waxed paper. Let sit until the chocolate is firm and set, at least 2 hours. Alternatively, insert the toothpicks in a sheet of Styrofoam and let sit until the chocolate is firm.

Chocolate-dipped fruit are best eaten within a day or two. Store in an airtight container, layered between sheets of waxed paper, in a cool, dry place. Refrigerate fresh strawberries.

Makes about 20 pieces   *Photograph page 87*

Chocolate-Rum Torte

1 cup cookie crumbs, from chocolate wafers or biscotti

2 tablespoons unsalted butter, melted

½ cup unsalted butter, at room temperature

¾ cup sifted confectioners' sugar

1 teaspoon vanilla extract

3 ounces unsweetened chocolate, melted and cooled

5 tablespoons rum, bourbon or brandy

1¼ cups heavy cream

2 tablespoons granulated sugar

4–5 slices sponge cake or pound cake, about ½ inch thick

1 tablespoon grated semisweet chocolate

The word *indulgent* readily comes to mind when describing this chilled, molded dessert. Serve with espresso or a rich, full-bodied coffee such as Estate Java, Sumatra or Colombia Nariño Supremo.

Preheat an oven to 375°F. In a small bowl, combine the crumbs and the 2 tablespoons butter. Press the mixture evenly into the bottom of an 8- or 9-inch springform pan. Bake for about 10 minutes. Cool completely.

In a large bowl, combine the ½ cup butter, confectioners' sugar and vanilla and beat until smooth. Beat in the chocolate. Add 3 tablespoons of the rum and beat until smooth and blended; set aside. In a medium bowl, whip the cream with the granulated sugar until stiff. Reserve 1 cup of the whipped cream. Fold the remaining cream into the chocolate mixture.

Spread half of the chocolate mixture over the crust. Cover with a layer of cake, cutting the slices to fit. Sprinkle the cake with the remaining rum. Spread evenly with the remaining chocolate mixture. Spread the reserved whipped cream on top and sprinkle with the grated chocolate. Refrigerate at least four hours, or overnight, before removing the sides of the pan.

Serves 8–10

Photograph page 90

Top to bottom: Chocolate-Rum Torte (recipe page 89), Caramel-Honey Nut Tartlets

Caramel-Honey Nut Tartlets

For the pastry:

1 cup all-purpose flour

2 tablespoons granulated
sugar

¼ teaspoon salt

½ cup chilled unsalted
butter, cut in 8 pieces

1 egg yolk

1½ tablespoons water

For the filling:

⅓ cup unsalted butter

3 tablespoons honey

¾ cup brown sugar, firmly
packed

3 tablespoons heavy cream

1 teaspoon vanilla extract

1 cup coarsely chopped
pecans or walnuts

1 ounce semisweet
chocolate, melted

If you like Southern pecan pie, you'll love these honey-sweetened tartlets.

Preheat an oven to 425°F. To make the pastry, place the flour, granulated sugar, salt and butter in a food processor fitted with the metal blade. Process until the mixture resembles coarse crumbs. In a small bowl, blend together the egg yolk and the water. Add to the flour-butter mixture and process until the dough forms a rough ball. Alternatively, place the flour, sugar and salt in a large bowl. Add the butter and, with a pastry blender or your fingertips, blend it into the dry ingredients until the mixture resembles coarse crumbs. In a small bowl, blend together the egg yolk and the water. Add to the flour-butter mixture and stir until the dough forms a rough mass.

Divide the pastry into four equal pieces. Pat each piece evenly over the bottom and sides of a 4½-inch-diameter tartlet pan with a removable bottom. To keep the pastry from becoming misshapen while baking, press a square of aluminum foil onto the pastry, molding it to fit snugly. Bake the pastry for 12 minutes. Lift off the foil and bake until golden, 3–4 minutes. Set aside.

To make the filling, combine the butter and honey in a heavy saucepan. Stir over medium-high heat until melted and blended. Add the brown sugar and stir until smooth. Bring to a boil and continue to boil, without stirring, for 2 minutes. Stir in the cream and vanilla.

Spread ¼ cup of the nuts in each tart shell. Pour the filling over the nuts. Bake until the filling is bubbling and has thickened slightly, 12–14 minutes. (Don't worry if the filling still seems runny; it will set as it cools.) Let the tartlets cool, then drizzle the melted chocolate over the top.

Serves 4–6

Chocolate Meringue Drops

2 extra-large egg whites

½ cup granulated sugar

6 ounces semisweet
chocolate chips, melted

½ teaspoon vanilla extract

½ teaspoon almond
extract

1 generous cup chopped
walnuts

Light little bites to serve with after-dinner or afternoon coffee, these are delicious with caffè mocha or, if you prefer, a light- to medium-bodied coffee from Costa Rica or Kenya.

Preheat an oven to 350°F and place a rack in the lower third of the oven. Cover two heavy-duty baking sheets with parchment paper.

In a small metal bowl, beat the egg whites, adding the sugar slowly, until the whites are stiff but not dry. Using a rubber spatula, carefully stir the melted chocolate, vanilla and almond extracts and chopped nuts into the egg whites.

Drop spoonfuls of batter, 1½–2 tablespoons each, onto the parchment paper and bake until the tops are dry, 12–15 minutes. Do not overbake. Cool completely in the pan before removing with a spatula.

Makes 1–1½ dozen cookies

Top to bottom: Chocolate Meringue Drops, Candied Citrus Peel (recipe page 94)

Candied Citrus Peel

6 oranges, grapefruits, lemons or limes

5 cups granulated sugar

2 cups water

2-inch piece of vanilla bean (optional)

Sweet crystallized strips of citrus peel provide a zesty nibble alongside caffè mocha or any other after-dinner coffee. Boiling the peel twice before candying it removes any trace of bitterness.

Thoroughly wash the fruit. Using a paring knife, cut off the stem and blossom ends of each fruit. Score the fruit from top to bottom into four or six segments. Remove the pieces of peel including the white pith.

Place the peel in a large saucepan, cover with cold water and bring to a boil. Simmer the peel, covered, for 15 minutes. Drain the peel in a colander, return to the pot and cover again with water. Simmer, covered, for another 15 minutes. Drain the peel in a colander and cut into strips ¼–½ inch wide.

Combine 4 cups of the sugar, the 2 cups water and the vanilla bean (if using) in a heavy saucepan over high heat and bring to a boil. Stir to dissolve the sugar. Add the strips of peel, reduce the heat and simmer until the syrup has almost disappeared, about 1 hour. Stir the peel and syrup occasionally to prevent scorching but take care not to break the peel. Remove the saucepan from the heat and transfer the strips of peel to wire racks to cool, about 20 minutes.

Place the remaining granulated sugar in a bowl. Roll the strips of peel in the sugar and set on a wire rack to dry, about 30 minutes. Store the candied peel in an airtight container.

Makes about 6 cups candied peel   *Photograph page 93*

ACKNOWLEDGMENTS

Sunset Books gratefully acknowledges the assistance and support of many friends at Starbucks Coffee Company: Howard Schultz for his incredible vision; and Howard Behar, Dave Olsen and Harry Roberts for making this book possible. We would also like to thank Shirley Bartlett, Derrick Chasan, Darlene Hartman, Tim Kern, Karen Malody, and all the Starbucks partners. We would also like to thank Peter Bang-Knudsen.

RECIPE CREDITS

Recipes by John Phillip Carroll: 46, 47, 50, 51, 53, 54, 55, 59, 60, 62, 65, 68, 69, 72, 79, 88, 89, 91
Recipes by Lora Brody: 56, 58, 64, 67, 70, 80, 82, 83, 84, 92
Recipes by Starbucks: 48, 74
Recipes by Sunset: 76, 78, 86
Recipes by Ruthanne Dickerson: 94

PHOTOGRAPHY CREDITS

The publisher would like to thank the following photographers and organizations for permission to reproduce their photographs:

(Abbreviations: b=below, t=top, m=middle, l=left, r=right)

Allstock/Louis Bencze 5
From the collections of Henry Ford Museum and Greenfield Village 9(b)
Lyons Ltd. Antique Prints 18–19
Nick Gunderson 4, 6–7, 20, 21(t), 21(b), 23, 29
Northwind Picture Archives 26(t), 28
Ann Rhoney 2, 10–11
Philip Salaverry 30–31, 34–35, 36, 37(t), 37(b), 38, 39, 40, 42, 43
Courtesy of San Francisco Public Library 8–9
San Francisco Museum of Modern Art, Bequest of Elise S. Haas 12
Stock Market/Denis Valentine 19
Tony Stone Images/Bruno De Hogues 8, Tony Stone Images/ Erik Svenson 14–15

The photographer and stylist would like to thank the following (from San Francisco unless otherwise specified): As You like It, New Orleans; Aude Bronson-Howard, NYC; Beaver Bros. Antiques; Bethanie Brandon Design; Biordi Art Imports; Cyclamen Studios Berkeley, Julie Sanders Designer; Decorum; Fillamento; Ward Finer; Bea and Marty Glenn; Nancy Glenn; Rosie Glenn-Finer; Interior Visions; J. Goldsmith Antiques; Mimi Koch Backgrounds; Merna Oeberst; Paul Bauer Inc.; Daniel Schuster; Sue Fisher King; Wilkeshome at Wilkes Bashford.